THE AWARE BEARS

We're Street Smart

A CHILDREN'S GUIDE TO STREET SAFETY

by
FRANK MACHOVEC
Director, Center for the Study of the Self
Richmond, VA

Project Director
JOHN DOWNEY

Project Coordinator
LOIS COHEN

Series Consultants
FRANK MACHOVEC, PhD
Licensed Clinical Psychologist
Director, Center for the Study of the Self
Richmond, VA

ALAN D. FRANKEL
Adjunct Professor, Westchester Community College
Valhalla, NY

THERESA STRELEC
North Castle Public Library
Armonk, NY

Illustrations by
KEVIN KLEIN

OCEANA EDUCATIONAL COMMUNICATIONS
DOBBS FERRY, NY

J362.7
Mᴀ

2038

Contents

Introduction: The Aware Bears   *iv*

We're Street Smart   1

Are You An Aware Bear?   26

Aware Bear Word List   27

Introduction: The Aware Bears

Have you ever seen a Panda before? May-Ling and Li Bear are Pandas. Pandas are cuddly, black and white bearlike mammals. They live in the bamboo forests of China. Pandas can be very big. They can grow to 5 feet tall and weigh 350 pounds. Pandas eat bamboo, roots, leaves, and flowers. They hold food with their feet and paws.

May-Ling and Li Bear are brother and sister. They live in a new place that is different from the bamboo forests of China. Living in this new place is fun. May-Ling and Li can meet new friends. They can go to school.

Like many other children, May-Ling and Li Bear need to be *Aware Bears.* Like Mommies and Daddies who love and care for their children, *Aware Bears* must love and care for each other and their friends. *Aware Bears* know what is good and what is bad. They know what is nice and what is not nice. An *Aware Bear* knows what to do when Mommy and Daddy cannot be there to help.

Be an *Aware Bear* and always be safe and well.

Li = L$\overline{\text{ee}}$

May-Ling and Mother Bear looked out the window and saw a police car stop in front of the house. May-Ling was surprised to see her brother Li get out of the car. A police officer took him by the hand.

1

May-Ling and Mother ran out of the house to meet them. "What happened?" Mother asked.

"Oh," Li said, "I got lost and this nice
police officer found me and brought me
home."

May-Ling gave her brother a big hug. "I'm glad he found you and you are safe and well. Tell us how it happened."

"I rode my bike to the park." Li explained.

"I was going to meet Pam and Polly at the
playground. It's a safe place. It has a
fence to stop balls from bouncing into the
street. There are safe things to play with
and to climb on. We had a good time on the
swings. We had fun running and
jumping."

"But Li, you know the park well. How did you get lost?" asked Mother.

"It was getting dark," said Li. "I knew it was time to come home. I thought I could find a faster way home, a better way. I rode and rode and rode on my bicycle, but could not find the way home. I was lost."

"Were you afraid?" asked Mother.

"I did not want to be," said Li. "But I know what to do when I cannot find my way. I must look for a police officer, a

helping friend, or a telephone. If I find a phone I should push 'O' for the OPERATOR. I should tell the operator that I need help."

The operator was very nice to Li. He asked
Li for his name. He asked Li where he
lived. The operator asked Li to tell him the
telephone number written above
the buttons on the phone.

He told Li to wait at the phone. A police
officer would come to help him.

The police officer had been parked across
the street from the telephone booth when
she got a call to help a lost boy.

The friendly police officer said, "I found Li far from home. I saw him ride his bicycle to the phone booth. He was riding his bike the right way, with the cars and buses. He was on the right side of the street."

May-Ling hugged Li. "It is good to ride your bicycle just like cars, in the same direction. It is different if you are walking. Then you walk facing traffic so you can see the cars and stay out of the way."

"Yes, I know," said Li. "On my bike, if I stop or turn I always give a hand signal. Others will know where I am going. If I do not give a hand signal I could turn into and hit a car. I could get hurt."

The police officer smiled at Li and said,
"You gave good hand signals. It was
dark; I could see your shiny safety vest.
You were very street smart to wear
something bright or light. Everyone could
see you."

"And remember, never cross a street
without looking carefully in every
direction," said May-Ling. "Always cross
at a street corner.

Bikes should have bright tape on them that shine in the dark. Bikes should run free and easy without problems. If they do not, you might have to leave your bike behind; carry it; or walk it back home."

"You are an aware bear, May-Ling," said
the friendly police officer. "Li, you should
know your neighborhood a block or two in
every direction.

As soon as you see strange or new things
you should stop and turn back. This way
you will not get lost."

May-Ling gave her brother another big
hug. "It's all right now, Li. The police
officer saw you and helped you.

The police are like Daddies and Mommies who care about us. They help us if we are lost."

The police officer smiled a happy smile. "I am glad I was there to help you Li. I am glad you are safe and happy.

I must go now, to watch out for others who
may be lost and who need help."

May-Ling and Li said goodbye to the police officer. They waved to her.

Mother gave her little bears a big hug.

"You are both aware bears. Daddy and Mommy love and care for you very much!" said Mother.

Are You An Aware Bear?

1| Why is a playground a safe place to be and play?

2| Name some places that are not safe. Why are they not safe?

3| What is the safe way to ride a bike?

4| Why is it important to have your bike run in good condition?

5| What is the safe way to cross a street?

6| What is the safe way to walk or ride a bike at night?

7| What is the safe thing to do if you are lost?

8| How can you keep from getting lost?

9| What bad things can happen if you do not follow safety these rules?

Aware Bear Word List

afraid   operator

aware   phone

bicycle   police

bike   problems

block   safe

booth   signal

bouncing   surprised

buttons   telephone

direction   traffic

explained   watch

neighborhood   written

KEVIN KLEIN
The Aware Bears "Youth-for-Youth" Illustrator

Sixteen-year-old **Kevin Klein** is a student at Hastings (NY) High School. In 1986, he was awarded first place in a Congressional Arts Caucus-sponsored art contest for high school students. In 1985, **Kevin** was one of only 150 New York students to be accepted into New York State's Summer School of the Arts Program at Fredonia College. **Kevin's** painting, *Portrait of Jenny,* is on display in Washington DC's Capitol Building as part of the Congressional Art Exhibit. One of his other works is on permanent display at the Albright-Knox Museum in Buffalo. Since 1978, **Kevin** has studied with artist Louise Freedman.

Kevin was selected from a group of youth artists to illustrate *The Aware Bears* series. During an introductory interview, each young illustrator presented his or her portfolio, discussed feelings on the need for safety education, and how he or she would approach the illustrating of *The Aware Bears* series. After these initial interviews, select artists were commissioned to illustrate a scene in watercolor. Each artist was given a detailed set of written specifications to illustrate. **Kevin** was selected on the basis of his ability to carry out these instructions, and for "bringing to life" May-Ling and Li Bear: THE AWARE BEARS.

Pearisburg Public Library

Pearisburg, Virginia

1. Books may be kept two weeks and may be renewed once for the same period, except **7 day** books and magazines.

2. A fine is charged for each day a book is not returned according to the above rule.   No book will be issued to any person incurring such a fine until it has been paid.

3. All injuries to books beyond reasonable wear and all losses shall be made good to the satisfaction of the Librarian.

4. Each borrower is held responsible for all books charged on his card and for all fines accruing on the same.